Jack's
Journey

Jack's Journey

Cecil Rhodes

WestBow
P R E S S
A DIVISION OF THOMAS NELSON

WestBow Press books may be ordered through booksellers or by contacting:

WestBow Press
A Division of Thomas Nelson
1663 Liberty Drive
Bloomington, IN 47403
www.westbowpress.com
1-(866) 928-1240

Because of the dynamic nature of the Internet, any Web addresses or links contained in this book may have changed since publication and may no longer be valid. The views expressed in this work are solely those of the author and do not necessarily reflect the views of the publisher, and the publisher hereby disclaims any responsibility for them.

Any people depicted in stock imagery provided by Thinkstock are models, and such images are being used for illustrative purposes only.

Certain stock imagery © Thinkstock.

ISBN: 978-1-4497-1141-2 (sc)
ISBN: 978-1-4497-1142-9 (e)

Library of Congress Control Number: 2011920425

Printed in the United States of America

WestBow Press rev. date: 02/07/2011

To Mom

Preface

It was after long deliberation and thought that I eventually sat down and wrote this book. I wrote for one reason—to encourage and inspire readers to stay the distance on the long and arduous road toward emotional healing. It is a long and difficult road to walk, but grace abounds along the way, and the journey is well worth it. I have detailed the places where grace is found so that others too may find restoration and renewal in these life-giving places.

I am indebted to two authors, Fr. Richard Rohr and Stephen Biddulph, for the wisdom and insight they provided me in their writings about rites of passage and initiation. Without their writings, I would not have been able to take this journey of healing.

Matthew and Robyn have walked the journey with me, and their constant belief in me and unconditional love are immeasurable.

Yviette has endured endless verbal and written editions of this book. Her love, patience, and encouragement have also been immeasurable. Without her by my side, none of this would have been possible.

Introduction

"And then one day you find ten years have got behind you,
no one told you when to run, you missed the starting gun."
(Pink Floyd, "Time")

This is Jack's story.

Jack wanted to tell his story because he thought he had something to say—something worthwhile and important; a message that needed to be heard. He didn't think the details of his story were that important, even though he loved the places and people in his life. In fact, he was very passionate about the people and places he loved. He just thought the message was far more important than the details, so he told his story without great emphasis on where and when it happened. He thought it much more important that you fill in your details and receive the message.

What Jack would want you to know about him is that he was a regular kind of guy, of average intelligence, with some talents and gifts, a positive outlook, optimistic on the whole, and a little more naïve than he should be. He loved sports and the outdoor life. These were his hobbies. You could add to his list of interests bird-watching and astronomy—in a very amateurish way, lest you think he was some kind of expert in these things. He loved reading, writing, and keeping a journal; that was how he expressed himself. He grew up alongside the ocean and loved the tranquility of water, always holidaying on the beach or near a lake or river. Spirituality was his real passion, and his library was stacked with spiritual books. He was never attracted to a career that built up financial resources. In this way you could say he was not very materialistic. He once heard a man described as a "minimalist"—that is, someone who chose to live a simple form of life—and he thought it summed him up pretty well. He didn't need a lot of things to make him happy, and to this day, he doesn't own that many things. He ended up doing what was his passion in life, and that was working as a pastor, among people and the spiritual life. He loved what he did. It did, however, take him a long time to get to this point of contentment. In the early days, he often felt frustrated and discontented. Until the difficult days began, Jack lived his life forward, always looking to the next thing that was going to happen and to a positive future. He still sees life like that, but he is far more content in the present now. He went through a ten-year period of looking back, reflecting, and fixing things in his life, and then he started looking ahead again.

Part One

INNOCENCE

Close your eyes have no fear; the monster's gone
he's on the run and your daddy's here.
(John Lennon, "Beautiful Boy [Darling Boy]")

Chapter One

THE EARLY YEARS

 ack was a child of the sixties. He quite neatly fitted the baby boomer profile of innocence, naiveté, and optimism. And he was the middle child! To him, being the middle child meant he could hang out with his older brother or younger sister, both options happily enjoyed. A happy child, the family maid who helped raise him later told him. "He was a happy child," she told his wife-to-be on a visit to his hometown to meet his father. It seemed more than he needed to get through life—a happy dispensation that he truly felt and an undying optimism that everything would be okay. It later blossomed into a vibrant faith that led him into a life in the ordained ministry of the church.

As a five-year-old, while visiting his grandparent's home, Jack was introduced to a talking frog called Freddie. Actually, it was his uncle sitting behind the wall of the front porch, but Jack didn't know that. The family was amazed he didn't figure it out, for Freddie was only there when his uncle was there and absent when his uncle was absent. They thought he would work it out, but he didn't. He long believed there was a talking frog called Freddie.

His spirit of optimism seemed natural, as though he were born with it—but no doubt the happy early years of his life contributed toward it. A bit of nature and a bit of nurture, as they would say. He grew up in a happy home, or so it seemed to him. Others may have seen it differently, but he saw it through innocent eyes, filled with optimism and self-belief. Later on in life—much later on in life—he would need to correct his worldview with a healthy dose of cynicism. But that is not how he grew up or how he saw the world. He was devoid of cynicism and sarcasm. He saw good in everything and everyone around him—an attribute he still has today. A natural talent in sport gave him popularity and acceptance among his peers, which was multiplied by an almost complete lack of killer instinct. He smiled in victory and he smiled in defeat, though he remembered a few stingingly tearful defeats along the way.

His was a busy life, with school and sports occupying his attention daily throughout the week and then sun- and sport-filled weekends. Hot, humid summers and warm winters meant he could be outdoors practically all year round. Only the summer rainfall prevented a day outside on the sports field, and these days were dreaded. If he wasn't playing soccer, cricket, or tennis, he went swimming in the sea or in a neighborhood pool. If that weren't enough to keep him off the streets, he would hang out at the local sports club where his parents spent most of their weekends. He would spend hours hitting a tennis ball against the wall or practicing cricket shots against imaginary opponents. He knew everyone in the neighborhood as well as they knew him. He was a likeable fellow, enjoyed as much by his pals as he was by their parents.

The house Jack grew up in had a conveniently placed courtyard—it occupied a central area of the house, below the bedrooms and running alongside the lounge. It was about twenty feet wide and thirty-five feet long, paved with slasto tiles. Along one side was a flower bed, which because his mother's frustration at seeing her garden ruined, was declared out of bounds. It was the arena of courtyard cricket and tennis! Fierce cricket test matches between South Africa, England, and Australia (he didn't know any other teams, as those were the isolated days of South African sport) were played on this patch of ground, as were the four major tennis tournaments—Wimbledon, the US Open, the Australian Open, and the French Open. Draws of sixty-four players were made, each and every player known to Jack and his older brother. If the cricket player or tennis player was left-handed, the homemade rules stated you had to play left-handed, too! Jack never recalls winning a game of tennis in those courtyard duels, as his older brother always had the edge on him. Whoever won got to choose who he wanted to be in the next round. To round these festivities off, his younger sister, who didn't get to play too much, proved to be a knowledgeable and competent commentator!

Being a child of the sixties, he and his pals played World War II games—the Germans versus the Allied Forces—or cops and robbers or cowboys and Indians. They listened to Elvis and the Beatles, once even forming a little band using cake tins, sewing needles, and tennis rackets as musical instruments. These were the days before television, when you made up the games you played and spent hours running around the neighborhood, climbing trees, building underground camps, and patrolling the streets— that is, if there weren't a tennis or cricket academy demanding your attention. It was fashionable to belong to a club or gang—you had to pass a test to attain membership and memorize a password to gain entry to the gang's tree house or underground camp. One Friday afternoon, Jack's gang met on the school playing field to fight another neighborhood gang. They would descend upon one another armed with sticks and tin rubbish bin lids. Looking back now, it seems quite barbaric, but at the time was actually harmless. No injuries were ever recorded in these battles to see whose gang was the strongest. Jack was the deputy leader of his gang, and to his horror, arrived that Friday afternoon to find the leader was not there. He had the responsibility of leading the gang into warfare. They got a whipping, and he recalls how he faked a broken arm to escape the wrath of the "enemy" as his gang fled in defeat. Legend has it that one of the boys once got tied to a tree in the small forest nearby and everyone forgot about him—that is, until it got dark and his parents sent a search party out for him. No one to this day remembers tying him to the tree where he was found later that night.

One of Jack's best childhood memories is of the endless tennis tournaments he and his brother played during the school holidays. Most of these were played in small country towns where they either stayed as guests of a local family, returning every year to the same family, or in the family RV, where his mom would oversee a number of teenage tennis players who all packed into the van and accompanying tent. Those were super times. Jack remembers how he and a friend sneaked into the local school boarding house where all the girls were staying—only to be discovered by the matron, who sounded the alarm and chased them out. Though his memory is vague now and the story verges on legend, he recalls how the night watchman of the boarding house threw a spear at them as they hastily clambered over the six-foot exit gate!

On another occasion, while staying with a local family at the Richmond Junior Tennis Tournament in Kwa Zulu Natal, Jack sneaked out late one night to go to a party some fourteen miles away in nearby Thornville. Somehow he and a friend managed to miss their ride back and ended up walking four and half hours on a very dark and lonely country road. He remembers climbing through the window into his room and laying his head down to sleep when the host of the house he was staying in woke him up for breakfast.

A highlight of the Richmond Junior was going for milkshakes at the ice cream shop on the main road. It was an old-fashioned ice cream shop with silver stools and big, round, red seats. Your milkshake was served in a tall glass, plus whatever was left in the stainless mixer it was made in. We enjoyed that free second serving!

Another legendary story revolves around the then-famous Michaelmas Invitation cricket week played in the October school holidays at Maritzburg College in Kwa Zulu Natal. Jack played for his high school first cricket team. The coach gave strict orders to the boys on their only free night out—no one was to go to the pub for a drink, and the ice rink was out of bounds. The previous year, the opening bowler had broken his ankle at the ice rink. The team duly set off on their free night out, half going to the pub for a drink and the other half venturing off to the ice rink, Jack in tow. He had no idea how to skate but figured it could not be too difficult. No sooner was he on the rink than he slipped over backwards and spread his hands to break his fall when another skater went straight over his hand. There was blood everywhere and a gashing wound on the top of his hand. His friends rushed him to a nearby hospital, got it stitched up and bandaged, and proceeded to make the long walk home. Hand in pocket, he smiled at the coach who was waiting patiently for all the boys to return. The next day, despite much protest, he was promoted up the batting order to open the innings. Thankfully, with a blood-soaked glove and in considerable pain, he did not bat for very long before he was given out caught behind and could return to the clubhouse for some respite. Maybe the coach knew a thing or two!

Back in Jack's childhood days, families still took three-week annual holidays. Every Christmas and New Year, stretching over three weeks, his family camped in their RV in the Drakensberg Mountain Range. The days were sun- and fun-filled, the sun only giving way to late afternoon thunderstorms, which when over would give way to sunshine again—except then the river streams cascaded over and the grass was soft and wet underfoot. Jack can still remember the fragrance and feel of the thick, green grass and the invigorating, gushing river water flowing over his head. He remembers rushing back to the RV to find a towel to dry while shivering in the late afternoon setting sun. Before television, cricket scores came via the transistor radio, which saw all the cricket fans crowded around, urging everyone to hush while an updated score was gathered. Cricket scores, card games, and storytelling were the order of the day if Jack and his friends found time for these pastimes in between horse riding, swimming, and hiking the mountain paths.

Chapter Two

GROWING UP IN THE ARMY

*W*hen Jack finished school, he—along with thousands of other young men—was conscripted to complete a year's military service in the South African Defence Force. It was a daunting prospect for him, for even at the tender age of seventeen, he realized he was part of an unjust system and faced the risk of fighting a war he did not believe in. Though he did not consciously process everything that happened that year, looking back, it was the beginning of a loss of innocence.

Despite the uncomfortable surroundings in which he found himself, he kept his indomitable spirit. He smiled his way through basic military training and all it involved. His life now belonged to someone else. Shaved hair and a brown uniform became the order of the day. Early morning inspections, near-impossible neatness and precision, physical training, marching, and weaponry occupied his daily attention. He learned to swear in another language, blaspheme endlessly, and drink inordinate amounts of beer. Jack and his new circle of friends coped with the meticulous and demanding routine of the military by adopting a carefree kind of attitude. Nothing was going to get them down, and they stuck together like glue. He remembers one particular day when his troop had run about ten miles in full uniform, with loaded backpacks and carrying a R1 rifle, only to be told when they reached their destination that they had to return to collect an item of clothing they had left behind. It was a ploy by the officers to break their spirit in the long and arduous process of building them into well prepared-soldiers—which when you saw this bunch of city kids in uniform looked like a near-impossible task. He was super-fit by then, and when the instruction was given to run a further ten miles, he and all the guys in the troop knew they could do it. A new comradeship sprung into life as they sang and ran their way back to where the run had begun a few hours earlier.

He was deployed in an artillery unit, the training of which was postponed as the unit trained as infantrymen preparing to do active duty on the Namibian and Angolan border. He grew up considerably that year. Five months of his life was spent patrolling the Namibian and Angolan border. The days were difficult, with a few scary and life-threatening moments. But at the end of the day, he completed the experience fairly well intact, certainly physically and pretty well emotionally sound. Others lost limbs and were emotionally scarred. Thankfully, he came out of it okay. Again that positive spirit and optimism came to his rescue. He didn't let too much of what happened and what he saw get to him. Instead, some great friendships were forged in those border camps, and the memory of comradeship and loyalty to his fellow man lingers still.

Jack's unit was split in two soon after its arrival on the border. The officer in command thought it wise not to have all these city boys together in one place too long, so he split their unit into two. Jack was in the group that moved a few hundred miles northwest to a camp near the great Ruacana Falls. He missed the friends he left behind but was delighted one day when the ration truck arrived laden with goods and he discovered, hidden under the load, his old friend Jacko. This typified their spirit and attitude—to make the best of the situation they found themselves in. Needless to say, Jacko returned, appropriately disciplined, to the base he had come from.

Most of their spare time was spent playing darts or soccer, two pastimes easily played in the confines and safety of the base. Occasionally, when time and security allowed, they would go swimming in the pools at the bottom of the Ruacana Waterfall. Shots were first fired into the water to scare off the crocodiles! Jack says he can't understand how stupid and careless they were back then—he sure wouldn't do that now.

An abiding memory of those days was the early morning return home from active military duty on the border. He hitchhiked the three hundred mile journey from his South African military base and arrived in La Lucia, Durban at 2:00 in the morning. He began to run the last few hundred yards along Durnford Avenue, hardly able to contain the mixture of relief and excitement to be back home. Before he could knock on the door to announce his arrival, the door flung open; his family had been sleeping lightly in anticipation of his return and had heard his footsteps coming along the road. Jack will never forget the bacon and egg breakfast that morning, the hot shower that followed, the excited chatter, and eventually the clean white sheets of his good old bed. The sun rose as sleep overcame him.

Soon he was back in the military base, finishing off the artillery phase of his training. He got lucky. The officers called on all A-grade math students to come forward. Only he and his pal Gary came forward, as this group of soldiers were not too bright. Actually, neither he nor Gary was that bright, either; they had fabricated the truth a little. They were actually both D-grade students. But they got the job of Technical Assistants, which they coped with admirably, considering. Even better was that they got out of all physical training, marching orders, and bad weather, spending all their time lodged safely and comfortably in their mobile office. Even the officers sought shelter, comfort, and a cup of hot coffee in their new home. It couldn't have got any better for them.

He completed his training two days after Christmas, and Jack—now eighteen years old and a licensed driver—was ready to take the world on. For the first time, he drove the family car on the highway, to the Drakensberg Mountains to join the rest of the family on their annual three-week holiday. At last, after a long year in the military, he was a free man—but more than that, he was now eighteen years old and a man in his own right.

Chapter Three

GROWING UP
AND GETTING MARRIED

At eighteen years old, Jack never really had any major career goals or aspirations. He had a natural flair for tennis and some talent, so he figured upon completion of his military training, he would join the South African tennis circuit in Cape Town, follow it to Port Elizabeth, and then play the last week in his hometown of Durban. That didn't materialize, as soon after he joined his family in the Drakensberg Mountains after completing his military training, he slipped and fell in the source of the Tugela River and tore the ligaments in his ankle. He hobbled home on crutches, bemoaning the lost tennis opportunity and also the inability to put his recently acquired motor vehicle skills to the test.

Following in the footsteps of his father and older brother, he registered for a business degree at the local university.

Still on crutches and waiting for the first term to begin, he was dragged off to the local Methodist church by his younger sister who had, in the year he was away from home and in the military, undergone a profound conversion experience. He loved what he found at the church, and a few weeks later, he too made a commitment of his life to follow Jesus Christ. It was a decision that changed the course of his life forever.

Though he had not grown up in a church environment, his family had instilled strong Christian values in him, and he felt that his conversion experience enabled him to give a more full expression to a whole lot of things that were in him already. Now he could name that which he had for long felt within. He had an innate spirituality, a sense of God in the world around him, knowledge of right from wrong, a compassion for people, and a love for creation. His conversion seemed a natural (though unexpected) experience. He jumped into the faith world enthusiastically, reading the Bible and spiritual books with great vigor and wholeheartedly getting involved in church and community life.

The seeds of what he was to do with the rest of his life were planted.

The years sped by. He eventually finished his business degree, married, and worked for five years in the accounting and auditing world. His first child, a son, was born.

A growing sense of call to ministry resulted in him taking up a post as an associate pastor at the nearby Westville Methodist Church, where he was to spend two happy and fruitful years.

A year in the mining town of Tsumeb in the north of Namibia followed as he began his formal training as a minister in the Methodist Church of Southern Africa.

Tsumeb turned out to be a place of significance for him. First, he discovered the power and longevity of suppressed memories and emotions. Driving into the town opened up a world of memory and emotion he had forgotten he even had. Sights, sounds, and smells filled his head as memories (not all them good) returned in a flood. He didn't even know the memories were there until his return to their place of origin. He was in the same place he had served as a young soldier eleven years before. His interest in the human psyche and the power of the unseen spiritual world deepened.

Secondly, he got a taste of mission work in a rural setting, which never left him. He looked after four congregations spread over a hundred-mile radius—the mining town congregation in Tsumeb itself, a group of Angolan refugees just outside the town in a village called Nomtsoub, a small group of farmers in nearby Grootfontein, and a host of young soldiers in various military bases.

The Angolan refugees made a lasting impression on Jack. Displaced overnight in the hot fire of conventional war, they had fled southern Angola into northern Namibia, not knowing who had survived and where their family members were. One in three was employed, but they formed new family units and shared equally among themselves all that was earned. No one was left out or better off than another. Once a month, Jack traveled the five and a half hour drive to Windhoek for in-service training. The congregation would take up a special offering for him to buy food on the journey. Jack protested and declined the gift, as he felt their need was greater than his. All he did was offend their dignity, and so each month, he graciously accepted their gift and learned much about the generosity of those whose lives had been fashioned in great adversity. They had a generous spirit far greater than his.

An unforgettable privilege followed Tsumeb when the dream of three years of full-time theological studies materialized. For three years, Jack ate, drank, and slept his studies. Mature age had made him a decent student, and for the first time in his life, he excelled academically. He remembers reading his textbooks in bed at night, so much did he lose himself in his studies! Student life was good to him. What the family lacked materially was more than made up with quality family time, low stress levels, and the forging of great friendships with fellow students. It was a time of profound learning and deep spiritual formation. Jack had finally found his life purpose and career path! His second child, a daughter, was born.

Jack was not very mechanically minded, so when his motor vehicle broke down on a hilly, remote road between Rhodes

University in Grahamstown and King Williams Town en route to fetch his sister from the airport in East London, the best he could do was pop the hood and watch in despair. To make matters worse, his four-year-old son vomited in the back seat of the car as he pulled over. No sooner had he pulled over than a Volkswagen Kombi pulled up to offer help. Jack was driving a Volkswagen Jetta. The help turned out to be a Volkswagen engineer from Germany traveling to King Williams Town to meet up with a South African Volkswagen engineer. Jack thought it was his lucky day. But it was to get better. The German engineer towed him into town, and despite Jack's protesting, took him to the South African engineer's home. The South African engineer decided to fix the car and offered Jack his car to fetch his sister from the airport and return home to Grahamstown. It was a lesson to Jack about the generosity of others and the providence of God, which he has never forgotten.

The fourth year of his degree was an internship year in a Cape Town congregation, a place Jack fell in love with. But he also fell into a ministry crisis. A beautiful place to live and a wonderful congregation could not cover up an inner doubt. Was he cut out for a life of full-time ministry? In between walking his Golden Retriever through the Tokai forest streams and taking long walks on the Noordhoek beach, he wrestled with the costliness of his call. He felt the life of call meant he had to be poor, busy, and righteous—three things that held little appeal for him. Long-distance running became a passion, and many a difficult issue was thought through on beautiful training runs. Jack and his running friends would run through Tokai, up Ou Kaapse Weg, down into Noordhhoek, and over Chapman's Peak and then meet the wives and children for a hot barbecued breakfast on the shores of Hout Bay. He completed three marathons that year, the most memorable being the Ford marathon—a most beautiful run from Green Point through the streets of Cape Town, around Devil's Peak, past Groote Schuur Hospital, through the southern suburbs, and along False Bay to end in Simons Town. It was also memorable, for he had run the last few miles straight into the infamous Cape Southeaster and vomited all the Coca-Cola he had drunk just two miles short of the finish line. He still managed to finish the race! The days were wonderful, but the niggle and doubt about full-time ministry lingered, and Jack decided to pack it all up and return to a life of accountancy in his hometown of Durban.

Jack was surprised how quickly he realized he had made a mistake. He remembers looking out of the window of the company he worked for, watching a gardener turn the soil, and feeling he was in the wrong place. He felt a bit like Jonah, the Old Testament prophet, whom God had called to Nineveh but who boarded a ship and went the other way. He too was going in the wrong direction. Cap in hand, he visited the presiding Bishop of the Methodist Church of Southern Africa to seek pardon for his rash and stupid decision to leave the ordained ministry. A pleasant surprise awaited him. The Bishop smiled, and with great joy in his eyes, said, "I've been waiting for you, welcome back!" They embraced, and later that year, Jack was ordained into the ministry of the Methodist Church of Southern Africa.

This saw the beginning of a golden period in his life. He was to spend the next fifteen years of his life in a large, flourishing church a few miles east of Johannesburg. Little did he know then that they would end in some considerable confusion and turmoil.

The golden years saw the church grow into a place of mission and ministry to the world around it. You just have to open the doors of a church in South Africa to step into a mission field, and the Edenvale Methodist Church did just that. An old hall and parsonage became a child care center and nursery school. It was the best in town and housed some 150 children and provided employment for twenty-three staff members. The Elton John Foundation sponsored the building of a hundred-seated soup kitchen, an ablution block, and an employment agency for unskilled workers. Across the road, an old house was converted into a fourteen-bed hospice for the poorest of the poor HIV/AIDS patients. It became a haven for people to die with dignity. This time, the sponsor was the film company DreamWorks. A DreamWorks social responsibility executive was in town one day, enjoying a cup of coffee at a local restaurant. He was searching for a HIV/AIDS projects to sponsor! One of the hospice workers was sitting at a table behind him, eavesdropping. She couldn't help noticing his blue eyes, and after listening to his conversation, she spontaneously and excitedly invited him to accompany her so she could show all the hard work we had done. We had poured every resource we had into the project and were near a breaking point, insolvency staring us in the face. DreamWorks invested, and the project was completed. On top of this all, the church ran the Alpha Course (a people-friendly, ten-week course seeking converts and attracting new members) four times a year, eleven years in a row. Hundreds of new members joined the church. Sunday services were full and vibrant. Thirty-five home groups blossomed as places of spiritual growth and pastoral care.

These were indeed the golden years.

Jack loved his life, his wife, his children, his Golden Retriever, and his two cats. He still had that innocent air about him—a touch naïve and still full of optimism.

Part Two

INNOCENCE LOST

"I thought Love would last forever. I was wrong."
(W. H. Auden, "Funeral Blues")

"Life is what happens to you while you're
busy making other plans."
(John Lennon, "Beautiful Boy [Darling Boy]")

Chapter One

FALLING APART AT HOME

It was soon all to end—the innocence, the naiveté, and the optimism. It all came tumbling down.

Jack was the last to know. Deep down in his heart, he knew it was coming, but he did everything in his power to avoid it. He denied it. He tried to fix it. He prayed and believed it would be okay. He wrote letters. He arranged dinners. He saw a counselor. He went away for a while to think. He did everything he knew how to fix it. But there was no fixing it. Divorce loomed large, and for Jack, the d-word was an unthinkable word. It had never ever occurred to him that his life would come to this. He thought love lasted forever, and so would his marriage. He was totally unprepared for what was to happen.

He tried not to show it. *Be brave and strong and true,* he said to himself—and in many ways, he was. But the truth was that he was shattered and did not cope well at all. He felt a deep sadness. Pain lined his eyes. This was not how he wanted it to be. Family stability and harmony were deeply ingrained in him. His family was the foundation of his life, and to lose it was devastating. He felt like he was in a vacuum of unreality, though if the truth is to be known, he was in reality like he had never known it before. Tears flowed easily, and the thought of being alone bore heavily upon him. He thrived in the security of home and family life. Home was the center of balance between work and recreation. Now home was in jeopardy, and Jack ached inside at this loss.

He knew all about the grief process—he had counseled many a bereaved person and many a divorcee—but he proved incapable of going through the process himself. He convinced himself he was going through it, and he tried to convince those around him, but the truth remained. He did not handle his loss well at all. It was not just the loss of the marriage, but the consequences divorce had on his family unit. Life was upside-down. Stability and peace, which he had known throughout his life, disappeared. All that was left was accumulated grief—and not just his, but his son's and daughter's. Anger, sadness, fear, anxiety, loneliness, and longing for relationship and comfort—all these things added up and hurt them more than they ever imagined it could.

Still, he carried on, keeping a smile and a brave face. *It will all work out eventually,* Jack thought to himself. Despite the sense of betrayal and disappointment he felt, he still believed he could heal and find the way forward again. What he didn't realize was that he was in denial—covering up the deep, sad feelings he had and moving on too fast. He could see it quite easily in others. Jack was steadfast in counseling to warn those in the same predicament as he to take it easy and be in no hurry to move on with their lives. But he couldn't see it in himself. Others saw this and pointed it out to him, but he was deaf to their love and care. The strengths of his personality—his naiveté and optimism—became his weaknesses. The personality traits that had gotten him so far became the very things that were to hinder him.

He became careless in his ways, careless in relationships, careless in his work, and careless in his commitments. His dependability weakened, and he started making poor decisions. He didn't see any of this at the time. Blinded by his grief and unaware of who he had become, he blundered on.

One relationship led to another, and one girlfriend gave way to another. It worried him somewhat, and he sought counseling again. He figured out he was going through what every forty-something divorcee was going through. To some extent, that was true—but it was also true that he had not resolved the loss of his marriage, and more importantly ,the loss of family, stability, and peace. He tried to cover these by finding love again—which he thought he did, and he remarried. Many voices cautioned him to slow down and take his time. But again, he didn't hear them. He justified his moving on by saying to himself that he had been single in his lonely marriage for a long time and that it was okay, therefore, to move on. Jack's second marriage was difficult and fragile, and it did not last long.

Chapter Two

FALLING APART AT WORK

*T*he turmoil took its toll on Jack, and soon holes were appearing at work. The once-flourishing church became conflict-ridden and difficult. One of Jack's strengths in leadership had been conflict resolution. He was fortunate to learn conflict resolution skills while studying at Rhodes University. An American conflict resolution expert had spent a sabbatical at the university, and many students, including Jack, were well trained in these skills. Jack had put them to good use, and the fruit was evident. However, in the turmoil and change of his personal life, he failed to lead as diligently and effectively as he had over the years. Tragically, like most things in his life at that time, he did not see it. Issues that he would normally deal well with became difficult, and the work situation deteriorated. Personalities clashed, and conflicts spiraled. People got hurt, and the ministry suffered.

Eventually, Jack moved to another church. He should have moved a few years earlier, while the going was still good. Much like a sportsman delaying retirement a year or two too long, Jack stayed a year or two too long. But the damage was done, and the golden years lost their gloss. He moved on, disappointed with the way things had ended. But still, a glimmer of that optimism remained for the next challenge that lay ahead.

But it was to no avail.

The move coincided with the failed second marriage, and Jack's ministry world collapsed. A twice-divorced minister, he thought, was an anomaly too much to bear. And he was right. He felt he had lost all integrity and dignity as a minster and that he had failed his calling. It was conveyed to him that he, Jack, was a decent enough person, but that as a minister, he no longer cut the grade. He understood the sentiment. Feeling like he did, he handed in his resignation. He did wonder, though, where he—Jack, the person—and Jack the minister began and ended. Were they one or two entities? *One,* he thought to himself—but he understood that many could not marry the two. Sadly and disappointedly, he began making plans to start another career. He had a business degree and would go back home and start all over again.

Chapter Three

HONEYDEW

A few years earlier, a wise old man had suggested to Jack that when he one day moved on from the Edenvale church, he should have a look at the Honeydew Baptist Church as a possible calling. Jack paid little attention to the suggestion other than to be puzzled why such a wise old man should make such an unlikely suggestion. Some time later, when divorce seemed inevitable, Jack was returning home from conducting a wedding out in the country. He was praying while driving and asking God for a sign. He was desperate, and when you are desperate, you ask God for a sign. As he said the word "sign," the headlights of his car illuminated a signboard ahead of him, which read, "Honeydew." The coincidence didn't go past him.

After handing in his resignation, Jack decided to rent a home for six months while he made plans for the next chapter of his life. He didn't leave himself much time to find a place and ended up urgently seeking suitable accommodation. A combination of limited time and budget narrowed his range considerably. He could not find anything suitable. Again, in desperation, he extended his search out into the country and immediately found just what he was looking for—in, of all places, Honeydew. In fact, at the time, he didn't realize it was Honeydew; he thought it was an extension of a neighboring area. It was only a few days later that his daughter pointed out to him that he was in fact in the place the old man had talked about and to which the signboard had directed. He wondered at the mystery of it all.

No sooner had he moved into the townhouse, which turned out to be perfect for him, than he received a phone call from the Bishop. He had dreaded the call, for it meant the finalization of his resignation. He was in for a surprise, though—for the second time in his life, he was on the receiving end of a gracious Bishop. "I have thrown your resignation away," the Bishop said to him. "Do you think you are a leper? We need to talk." Jack replied in the affirmative. Yes, that was exactly how he felt. He felt his marriage failure had excluded him from his calling and his work. He felt embarrassed—a dismal figure in the public eye, no longer able to keep his dignity and honor to that which he had been called. The only right and noble thing to do was to resign and get on with his life by focusing on another career. The Bishop's phone call changed all of that. Jack was given six months of compassionate leave and the opportunity, once he had met the church's pastoral and disciplinary requirements, to continue in the ordained ministry.

He found himself in the strangest of circumstances. He was without the things that defined him for so long. He no longer had the things that made him who he was—no ministry, no marriage, no status—minimum wage and lost respect now defined who he was. He didn't know what to do with himself. It was time-out. On top of it all, he felt down and discouraged. He thought he had hit the bottom some years earlier, but this was worse. It seemed to continually go from bad to worse—one poor decision after another and a struggle to keep it altogether. Jack spent many a day and night sitting alone on the porch, contemplating the downward spiral of his life and wondering if and how he would get it back together again. He sometimes wished he were not a minister in the public eye, running in the headlights for all to see and pass judgment and wonder what was happening to him.

Then the strangest thing happened to Jack. He began to find himself. The old, optimistic Jack started to return. He now had lost the naiveté that had for so long shaped his personality. The innocence of his youth had disappeared, and a more balanced and mature man emerged. It had been a long and costly journey to bring him to this place.

Less was now more for him. The accumulated losses, which had befallen Jack, left him in a simpler place than he had ever been before. Simplicity and inactivity became the order of the day. Hours of nothingness and solitude drove him to a deeper examination of himself and of life. He was driven to God's way of working in the difficult things of life.

It was strange, too, because he never felt totally comfortable in the place of nothingness. And at the same time, he never felt that he had progressed far enough to say he had resolved the issues of the past. He was constantly in between. He was learning to live in the moment of uncertainty and trust it would get him to where he should be.

Honeydew became a time of waiting—a place of formation of something new and something better.

$\mathscr{P}art\ \mathscr{T}hree$

AMAZING GRACE

"Here comes the rain again, falling from the stars,
drenched in my pain again, becoming who we are."
(Green Day, "When September Ends")

FIVE YEARS LATER ...

$\mathscr{I}$t was five years after Honeydew that Jack wrote down the story of his life. That was not as important to him as what had transpired in him in coming to terms with divorce and the tremendous inner struggle and sense of failure it brought to him personally and at work. He figured everyone had a story to tell; the facts and details were different. But he was not sure if or how everyone worked it all out. He felt compelled to write down an account of his spiritual journey that brought him to a place of understanding, healing, and wholeness, where he could hold his head high again and continue his life and ministry with dignity. He felt the need to write his story down, for he knew how difficult the road is to walk. He felt God put his feet back on higher ground, and he wanted to share with others, in some detail, what that journey was like for him. He never felt like he had all the answers, but he did feel he had something to say about what he discovered along the way about himself, life, and God.

He found the resources he needed, mainly in four places. He found mountains of wisdom and insight on a brand-new journey for him in the ancient world of rites of passage and initiation. He turned to biblical stories and rediscovered another ancient truth—the people of God walked long and winding roads on their faith journeys, facing the same complexities, confusions, and failures he did. He found, to his surprise (the naive side of him), judgment and alienation in the church—much more than he did outside of it. In the same breath, he found in the church also what he believed the church was all about—grace upon grace. Lastly, he found amazing strength and self-belief in the love and loyalty of family and friends.

Chapter One

INITIATION AS GRACE

A few years before Jack began his downward spiral, he received the gift of a book by Stephen Biddulph called *Manhood*. It was one of those books that sat forgotten on the bookshelf for a few years. One day, he picked it up and started reading it, and he could not put it down. The book inspired him and opened up a world of understanding he had never seen before. He read the book several times over the span of a couple of years, devouring its wisdom and finding a way to interpret his life.

No words spoke more to him than these:

> Young men need to fall before they can rise. Adolescence is not the big transition. No one is even close to being a fully-grown male before they turn forty! Charming and cocky in their twenties and thirties, men think they are invincible. Eventually (mid-thirties?), all men learn not everything works out in life. Shame, error, and grief

[are] all around. Welcome to the Ashes. You do not have to experience total devastation in order to grow into a mature man, but you have to know its possibility deep in your bones—to discover that you are not all-powerful and your dreams may well not come true. Thus you may make the journey down into Ashes, perhaps many times. Finally you get the message and only then do you go from being a careless boy to a more openhearted and compassionate man. Every man needs an ashes time in his life. To discover that, in spite of all optimism and effort, one is still vulnerable. Life is about going on, being active, making decisions, taking steps in this life, not knowing how it will work out. Life is a tough business. If a man is able at these times to allow himself to cry and share some of his pain with his friends, then he comes through a better man. His capacity for compassion deepens enormously. The Ashes time completes what began in adolescence—the making of a real man. Accept times of great misfortune—a marriage breakdown, sickness, or business failure—as essential steps to getting free. Roll in the ashes. Don't be afraid of pain, grief, sadness, weakness, or failure. They enrich your humanness. [1]

Jack had never heard such thinking before. Certainly no one had ever spoken to him about these things. He thought you were expected to be a full-grown, mature male by your mid-twenties, and that if things went wrong, you were doing something wrong. Somewhere along the line, he developed the idea that you had to get things right and that you measured yourself by your successes and achievements. Somewhere in the back of his mind, this idea still lurks. He was not sure if this had something to do with the world of success and achievement he grew up in or if it had something to do with the morality of the religious world he had become a part of. Certainly these two messages combined and all but dulled out any other message of how life should be.

Here was a voice saying something different, and it made the world of sense to him. He developed an insatiable appetite to find out more about it.

He discovered that this thinking was rooted in the ancient practice of young males going through well-identified rites of passage to initiate them into the adult world—not to just to make them adults, but also to prepare them for the eventualities of adulthood. It fascinated him, challenged him, and most significantly, introduced him to a way of understanding his life journey and making the most of the circumstance he found himself in. No, not just making the most of his circumstances, but acknowledging the inevitability and necessity of the adversity he faced and allowing it to do what it must to make him the man he must be.

"Roll in the ashes. Don't be afraid of pain, grief, sadness, weakness or failure. They enrich your humanness." *Wow,* Jack said to himself, the exclamation a long time in the making. These words were life to him. "Thus you may make the journey down into Ashes, perhaps many times. Finally you get the message and only then do you go from being a careless boy to a more openhearted and compassionate man."

At this time, he came across another author and thinker who was to radically challenge him on his initiation as grace journey—Fr. Richard Rohr, a Franciscan priest of the New Mexico province.

Fr. Richard Rohr said similar things as Stephen Biddulph, and Jack soaked it all in. It made all the sense in the world to him, and he allowed the words to sink deeply into his consciousness and shape the person he was becoming. He began to thank God for the falling in his life rather than resent it and question it. He now understood why it was there.

> The state of the male species is not good. Men like roles instead of process, dressing up instead of dressing down. The male has to be taught. Almost all ancient cultures recognized this and therefore deemed initiation necessary for the survival of the tribe. The male must be taught the "tears of things" before you can invest in him power, or he will always abuse that power. Initiation is always an intentional journey into powerlessness, so the man will know how to use power well. Our young men are taught that life is about job, role, security, placement, and advancement—about being in control. The pattern of ascent is so in their hard wiring of the male that cultures knew they had to teach the male *at the beginning* the crucial and necessary knowledge about descent. Initiation. It was too late to tell him about it after he had put twenty years into climbing, achieving, and promoting himself. Initiation tells you, you are going to have to build your tower, yes, but have no doubt that you must also descend from the tower you have built. And the higher you build it, the more defeats and humiliations you will need. [2]

More defeats and humiliations? Yes, Jack understood this, and he began to learn from his initiations.

Fr. Richard Rohr also introduced Jack to the concept of liminal space—liminal, from the Latin word *limen,* meaning "a threshold"—the place where you are betwixt and between, where there is loss of control over your circumstances and destiny. It is in this place where transformation best happens. The place where the trapeze artist finds himself in the moment both hands have let go of the bar—he is betwixt and between. It is a risky place to be but a place of profound transformation. Jack found himself coming back to this place again and again until he had learned the lessons—until transformation had taken place.

What struck Jack was that these life lessons were all learned in the adverse circumstances of life. He learned to befriend the pain and confusion, the lostness he felt, and to learn from it rather than question himself about it or wonder what he was doing wrong to attract it. He learned not to listen to the judgment of others about who he was—and there was plenty of that, especially among those in the religious world he lived in. He began to see these things as allies rather than as enemies. Fr. Richard Rohr put it in these words: "And so initiation is hid in our bodies—it is in our human flesh, our human experience, our life journey itself. This we can never escape. All we need to do is listen to our lives and learn from them. We all have lives and bodies. It levels the playing field, and I have slowly learned to trust that I get what I need to learn the necessary lessons." [3]

Jack also learned that that the idyllic and safe world that he grew up in was, to a large extent, a false world. The naiveté and optimism he had needed to be corrected by a healthier dose of reality. This is not to say it is wrong to grow up in a safe and naïve world, but it is to say there needs to be correction somewhere along the line.

As Jack made the corrections he needed to, he developed a great interest in the ancient rites of passage that young adult males experienced as initiation. He wondered what they were, how they worked, and what had happened to them in the modern world. His son and daughter were on the verge of young adulthood, and he wanted them to learn the things he had not learned. He recognized that their upbringing was nowhere near as uneventful as his. They had been exposed to pain, loss, and confusion at a far younger age than he, but now he took comfort in the fact that if they learned the lessons at a young age, they would be more prepared for life than he was. And so he began to experiment with ancient rites of passage in the modern western culture he lived in.

He discovered in the writings of Fr. Richard Rohr three essentials of an ancient rite of passage:

They are sacred. "Private discovery of meaning is not enough. There has to be some collectively agreed upon 'sacred.'" [4]

They are ancient. "What makes ritual powerful and effective is that they have been done by our ancestors and can be tied up with our archetypal imagery of the Great, the Good, the Holy." [5]

They are communal. "There must be a community that shares this meaning and that initiates with conviction and ongoing intent." [6]

These three essentials of a rite of passage, together with Stephen Biddulph's understanding of the role of the wilderness in an initiation, formed the basis of an experience Jack put together to discover the power of initiation in the lives of young adults. The wilderness is the basis of all ancient rites of passage. We can never underestimate our need, as men, for wilderness—in the wind, under the stars, and in the crash of the waves. Jack needed no encouragement to include the wilderness. He loved the outdoors. He had hiked many a trail in and around Southern Africa, including the Fish River Canyon in Namibia (twice), the Blyde River Canyon, the Titsikama, the Amatola, the Alexander, and the Reebok. It was on the famous Otter trail that he broke his leg and ankle, which later led to a massive pulmonary embolism. To add to that, he had run several marathons, scuba dived in the Comores, and walked through the Kruger National Park. He remembers how on one of the wilderness trails, his family had hugged a giant ancient fig tree and felt its power and warmth. He felt akin to creation and longed to feel its power in shaping lives.

Three times, Jack took groups of young adults and their parents into the Pilanesberg wilderness to go through specially designed rites of passage to initiate the young adults. Though the ancients only initiated the males, Jack felt that in today's modern world, females should be initiated, too. Fr. Richard Rohr concurred:

Most ancient cultures did not feel the need to initiate women. Only her capacity for fertility needed to be blessed and affirmed. Once a woman has gone through the experience of a totally new body coming out her body, she knows the biggies and the essentials. She knows something about the inherent connection between suffering and new life, she knows that it happens through her and yet also totally in spite of her, she knows something that a man simply does not know about mystery, miracle, darkness, and waiting. Ideally, the woman understands transformation and therefore has a basic head start in understanding spirituality. She knows (if she is listening, that is), whereas he has to be taught, he has to be carefully taught. [7]

And to make matters worse most young women are now buying the same delusion and calling it liberation. This new generation of women, who have every right to build their tower, will now need the same classical initiation and will have to suffer their own turn on the downside of the wheel of fortune. [8]

Using the three essentials of an ancient rite of passage, Jack designed the initiation experience around wilderness, water baptism, and a sacred meal. All three had ancient roots and were sacred. Still today, he has struggled to gain some kind of communal buy-in. *Perhaps,* he thought to himself, *this is why rites of passage and initiation are no longer practiced today, for there is no communal agreement about these things.* Our world is too cosmopolitan and secular to find a common mind on these things. He was not sure how this could happen other than in the small community he built around what he was doing—which, to this day, has not transpired. He added to the three rites of passage a fourth exercise, and though not technically a rite of passage, it nonetheless had a great impact on the experience, and that was to teach young adults and parents to listen to each other in ways they perhaps had not listened before.

This recorded, in-depth dialogue from one of the wilderness trips Jack took illustrates the power of listening, which the great theologian, Paul Tilllich, described as the first step in loving.

> The first skill they learned was to decide who spoke first! One would speak while the other listened. This turned out to be hilarious. No one had communicated in this way before. They were used to both parties speaking at once, each defending their position, each thinking of what they were going to say next, each expressing an opinion or judgment ... and not really taking the time to listen. So they were taught to listen. Imagine you were crossing a border. You check in your passport, and you enter as a guest of another country—another world of sounds, sights and delights. You are in that world now, not yours. Think of listening in this way, they were taught. Get into the world of the one speaking and listen to what they are saying, not what you are thinking. The skill needed to do this is called mirroring. You simply repeat back what you heard. Simple? Oh no, this skill was learned with great difficulty. It took them some hours to begin to undo the unhealthy ways they had learned to communicate. Richard and his eighteen-year-old son, Jeff, had volunteered to be used as guinea pigs modeling how to use this skill of mirroring. Jack had asked them to use a fairly low-key issue to talk about. Jeff asked if he could speak first. They agreed. "Dad" he said, "when I get home in the early hours of the morning after a night out on the town, I get the feeling you think I have been out drinking and getting up to no good. It feels like

you don't really like the way I am, and you don't really trust me." Wow, Jack thought to himself, I asked them to talk about a low-key issue in their lives! Now Jeff was quite different to his Dad. He wore his hair long, had several rings piercing various parts of his face, and his jeans hung halfway down his hips.

Richard didn't hear a word Jeff had said. He was still in his own country! He vehemently disagreed with Jeff and told him so. Jack interjected, asking Jeff to repeat what he had just said and for Richard to simply repeat back what he heard. Again, Richard got it wrong and expressed his opinion of what his son had just told him. He wasn't listening. He was too busy formulating his response, making his judgments, and expressing his opinions to hear his son. The third time, Richard got it right and mirrored back what he heard. It was a defining moment for father and son. For the first time in a long time—maybe the first time ever—Richard listened to his son. As he mirrored the words "you feel like I don't really like the way you are," he realized that was how his son perceived him. Yes, it was true; he said, "That is how I make you feel, I am sorry, tell me more." The two of them never looked back. They spent hours and hours listening to each other.

The second skill is to summarize all that was said. This is just to make doubly sure that the one listening got it all right.

Then the hard work began. The one listening needed to be sure he understood what he had just heard. It is a great skill to have listened—to have really listened—without interruption, without expressing an opinion, without thinking what you are going to say next, without making a judgment. It is another thing to have understood what you just heard. So the one who has listened says, ""What you say makes sense to me because …" This is to validate what was said—to confirm with the person that what they had been saying made sense.

And it got even more difficult. The next step in listening was to say, "I can imagine this is how you might have felt ..."—in other words, to empathize with what you had just heard, to try and get into the feelings of the other person Richard got this right first time. He said to Jeff that he would imagine this might have made him feel hurt and rejected. Yes, Jeff said to his dad, that was exactly how he has been feeling. The listening that first began when Richard accurately mirrored back to Jeff what he had heard culminated when Richard reflected back to him how this all might have made him feel. It was as though when Richard understood Jeff's feelings, he understood Jeff. They had come such a long way in such a short space of time. It almost seemed staged. How could such a profound moment between father and son happen so quickly—at such depth?

One morning, in the Pilanesberg Game Reserve, Jack's daughter woke everyone up with a very loud whisper! "Lion," she shouted in a hoarse whisper. The entire party shot bolt upright out of their sleeping bags, the two wilderness guides the first to stand and take stock of what was happening. There, some one hundred yards away, stood two lions. They casually observed the party camping under the fig trees, unaware of the turmoil they were causing. Excited and nervous chatter prevailed over breakfast, and when the day's trail began, there was a great deal of trepidation and wondering. How many more were out there?

The trail party walked in a straight line—the two guides up front, with Jack bringing up the rear. Jack recalls looking behind his back to see that all was clear many times on the trail! The reason the two guides led up front was in the unlikely event of gunfire—no one would be caught in the crossfire. And it was an unlikely event, as such trails had a perfect safety record. The guides were professional in all they did; they were conservation lovers who carried weapons only for use in the event of an extreme emergency. An hour or two of walking and seeing nothing surprisingly undid the nervousness of the earlier sighting of the lions. The group became more relaxed as the day wore on—that is, until one of the guides stopped abruptly in his tracks, raised his hand in a gesture to stop, hurriedly took a few steps back, and fell over a rock. The first thing Jack noticed from the back was that the guide fell over, and he was perplexed as to what was happening. Then the entire party saw the danger. Some thirty yards away, in the shadow of a tree, stood a black rhino. Black rhinos tend to be more aggressive than white rhinos and are known to charge if they feel provoked. The group walked upwind from the rhino, and due to the rhino's poor eyesight, it did not see or smell the trail party. Whispered instructions ordered the party to retreat quietly and slowly, being always on the lookout for a tree to climb should the rhino charge. There were twelve in all and about five decent trees, which meant survival lay with the fastest runners! While the party was retreating, the rhino let out an ear-piercing scream, and dust flew in the air as another unsighted rhino charged and attacked the rhino the party was retreating from. Seconds of confusion and panic set in, as it was difficult to tell exactly what was going on.

Thankfully, the battling rhinos fought off each other at incredible speed in the opposite direction.

What Jack discovered on these wilderness trails was the amazing power of the rite of passage. It was mind-boggling what the young men and women learned. The learning was written in their hearts forever, he felt. The rite of passage did what a million words, lectures, and sermons could not do. The young adults were initiated. Sleeping under the stars in the tracks of the African wildlife, going down under the water to symbolically drown and come up again, encountering wildlife on their terms in their environment, and eating a sacred meal prepared together powerfully spoke into their lives. They learned that they were not in control; how vulnerable life actually was; that they would go down but rise again; how they were connected to the universe, creation, and the ancients; how the elders collectively spoke wisdom into their lives; and how safe they actually were in the place of abomination.

These amazing life lessons were learned with few words spoken.

The parents overseeing the process and the wilderness guides leading the trail were not left untouched—nor was Jack. They were all processing these things, recognizing their own personal need to be initiated so as to understand what life had already delivered to them. The one particular piece of water was up in the hills and freezing cold. Jack went in first and wondered if anyone else would brave the cold to join him. By the end of the experience, they were all in the water, each taking a turn to go down under the dark, cold water (a powerful symbol)—young adult, parent, and wilderness guide, they all went down, some understanding what was to come while others interpreted what had already happened.

Jack came out of these experiences processing all that had happened to him, how necessary and inevitable these things were, and how his falling was making him a better man. He rolled in the ashes of his life. He gave thanks to God for keeping him safe and doing a deep work in the abominations of his life.

Through rites of passage and initiation, Jack found grace upon grace—grace that was more than sufficient for his life.

Chapter Two

BIBLICAL GRACE

While reading for his theological degree, Jack loved biblical studies. He ended up majoring in New Testament Greek, but such was his interest in the Old Testament that he could have easily majored in Old Testament Hebrew.

Old Testament studies were generally regarded as tougher than New Testament studies, and it showed in the exam results. Every Friday, the students wrote a harrowing time test. If you got through that, you would get through the final exam.

He remembers one particular class.

The book of Daniel was before the class when an extremely angry and grieving student walked in, and in strong language and with great emotion, wrote off the book of Daniel as rubbish! "People die in the lion's den, and they burn in the furnace!" he exclaimed. The God of his family did not protect them at the hands of the South African Security forces. What God was this that saved some people from violence but allowed others to die? The security police had murdered members of his family, and he wore his grief and burning anger on his sleeve.

Then began the most profound lecture Jack had ever heard. The Doctor of Old Testament studies explained how Daniel was written some three hundred years after the events of the 587 BC exile in which it was set. The time during which it was written was the terrible persecution and near elimination of the people of Israel at the hands of the Seleucid King, Antiochus IV Epiphanes. Daniel told heroic stories of bravery and resistance of the exilic time to inspire the people to stand fast in the persecutions they were facing. You could decide for yourself if these were miracle stories or stories of hope in adversity. We made up our minds easily that day. People die in acts of violence, but the human spirit and resolve to triumph in adversity never does. God was with his family in the evil persecutions they faced, and he would see them through it all—even though it came at the sacrificial cost of many human lives. The South African story went on to vindicate all that we learned that day.

Old Testament studies introduced Jack to the triumphal nature of the human spirit when in relationship with God. He saw how humane and ordinary the great men and women of God were. Their deeds were ordinary; their faith in God was extraordinary. Their life stories were littered with failure, deceit, betrayal, intrigue, drama, and uncertainty. But they were also littered with bravery, loyalty, devotion, passion, and obedience. They walked a long obedience in the same direction, every now and then straying off the path, but always finding their way back to it.

In his difficult days, Jack readily identified with the Old Testament characters. They seemed just like him!

Abraham left behind his known world, family, and friends and set out into a foreign land, trusting in the promise of God. He faced famine, traded his wife as his sister, allowing the King of Egypt to take her as his wife, quarreled with his nephew, Lot; and split ways with Lot, each going in different directions—and that was just the beginning of his story. Abraham negotiated many an unexpected twist and turn and many a difficulty before he overcame.

Joseph was left in a pit to die, then instead sold to slavery in Egypt, his death faked to explain his absence to his father. He was then sold as a slave to one of the Egyptian king's officers, where he thrived. What a story line! Successful in all he does, he is blessed by God, only to be betrayed by Potiphar's wife and imprisoned on false charges. God's blessing remains with him, and we know the rest of the story. Grace dominates his life.

Moses, subversively raised by his slave mother and then adopted by the king's daughter, grows into an angry young man, kills an Egyptian in an outburst of anger, and flees for his life. He starts another life in the desert, marrying into Jethro's family. God divinely appears to him and calls him back to face his fears and inadequacies, return to Egypt, and free God's people from slavery.

Jack fully identified with the stories of these great people of faith.

Elijah, exhausted, takes refuge in a cave. The honor due to him dissipates into fighting for his life.

King David faced betrayal, deceit, adultery, and murder. On the run from his enemies and on the run from God, it takes Nathan, the prophet, to bring him to his senses.

Obscure and unlikely candidates—Tamar, Rahab and Ruth— make it into the bibliography of Abraham's descendants.

New Testament stories build on the Old Testament.

Nathanael, Nicodemus, the women at the well, the women caught in the act of adultery, Matthew, the tax collector, the sons of Zebedee, Simon (later to be called Peter), Judas (the one called Iscariot), Mary Magdalene, the hemorrhaging women, the Roman officer, the paralyzed man, the lame man, the blind beggar, Bartimaeus (son of Timaeus), the ten lepers, Zacchaeus, and the list goes on—this is the Biblical story, a wonderful tapestry of grace upon grace.

Jack took great comfort and strength in this biblical picture of grace.

It was for him as Paul described: "For it is by God's grace that you have been saved through faith. It is not the result of your own efforts."

There was no guile in Jack, and his intentions were good. He knew that. His heart was a heart after God's; it had always been like that. Like that of King David, his heart was in devotion to God, and he aspired to live well.

Another way of understanding the biblical grace on his journey was to hold together the extremes of suffering and shalom. Jack understood the inevitability of things going horribly wrong—sickness, death, bankruptcy, war, natural disaster, divorce, and addiction—as testified in the biblical story. It is the common theme of both the Old and New Testaments. Suffering threads its way throughout the story, especially personified in Israel, Jesus, and many others as you read their witness. The biblical witness of suffering is to cry out to God for help, and to thank God for the transformation and renewal suffering can bring. This is much easier said than done. Jack's experience as a pastor for over twenty-five years is that for as many who experience their suffering as redemptive, there are many who experience their suffering as destructive. Nonetheless, suffering is an integral part of the biblical story. On the other hand, so is shalom—peace, prosperity, health, and abundance. The word *blessing*, which is associated with shalom, means to be exceedingly happy. Both the Old and New Testaments promise shalom and blessing. God's plan for Israel in the midst of their suffering, according to Jeremiah, was not disaster but prosperity. Jesus said the thief came to steal, kill, and destroy, but he came to give abundant life.

If Jack applied this biblical norm to his life, then he should expect to both suffer and be blessed—and to bear the consequences of both. Suffering is like the furnace, producing a fine, finished product—and shalom, after suffering, brings joy to life and a greater sense of responsibility to use the blessing which you have received wisely and generously.

Chapter Three

THE CHURCH
AS A PLACE OF GRACE

O n the whole, Jack would describe his experience of the church as a place of grace, which he always thought it should be. Two Bishops and countless other colleagues, friends, and congregants bestowed upon him unconditional love and underserved merit.

This was, however, shadowed somewhat by some who chose to judge and others who chose to feast on a scrumptious diet of rumor and gossip. Jack knew the damage the tongue could do, and he experienced it firsthand. The real difficulty came with half-truths and truths just slightly twisted and taken out of context. He had seen that play out in the newspapers, in the movies, and in the lives of public figures; now he saw it play out in his life. At times he handled it well, and at times he let it get to him, resulting in endless introspection or needless retaliation, neither doing him any good.

This aroused the question in Jack as to how God worked in situations like these. Was judgment an integral part of the journey? Israel were judged by God in exile before he comforted its people and brought them back home, as the first few verses of Isaiah 40 describe. Perhaps judgment was not only integral, but also the inevitable result of bad decisions and a necessary step in the journey of healing and salvation? Jack wondered about these things.

Jack was familiar with the concept of biblical judgment but had never really paid much attention to it. He tended to focus more on God's attributes of grace, mercy, and forgiveness. That is how he saw God, and he was hesitant to blur this picture with the picture of a judgmental God, which he saw as harsh. He now sees that there were some adjustments he had to make regarding judgment and the role it can play in life. "Judge not, lest you be judged," a saying Jack lived by, was very different than God's judgment in an individual's life. Jack didn't regard himself as a scholar or intellectual on these matters, but he felt his life experience, biblically interpreted, was telling him something he had missed. Being a twice-divorced minister with a messy and confusing long-term ministry ending has consequences. Was this just another way of saying there is judgment? This is not to say he was beyond redemption—not at all. Rather, it is to say that judgment is a necessary journey on the road to redemption. Actually, in a roundabout way, is an important step in grace, in God's loving yet disciplined actions in one's life?

Could it be, Jack wondered, years after the events took place, that the difficulties he experienced were all a part of God's judgment, an inevitable part of the journey? Years later, he is certainly more at peace with it and can see, despite the agony he felt at the time, that it did force him to reflect, with a greater honesty, on all that happened to him. He has let go of the part which was gossip and rumor and focused more on the part that he needed to face and deal with.

Today, Jack sees the actions of the church and its leaders as grace in his life. The good and the bad experiences, the clear and the confusing moments, all led him to the place of grace. He wants to shout out loud that it is a long, painful, and difficult journey! It took years. His journey was one of self-doubt, fear, anxiety, and shame on the one hand—and on the other hand, a journey of hope, salvation, love, and discovery. If the church were not there to hold the checks and balances—to say the things no one else could say—would one be able to arrive at a place where the restorative work is done? Now Jack would answer this question by saying that no, the work could not be done without the stern and painful examination of character the church required of him.

Jack's still not sure when this salvation journey he has been on ends—when you can close the chapter and move on. He suspects you can't—it is an ongoing, constant journey of growth and healing. But what he did see is that his life moved on and new doors of opportunity presented themselves. As he walked through those doors, he slowly rediscovered his passion, dignity, and call.

Another anomaly Jack thought could describe this tense relationship between judgment and grace was the Latin phrase *felix culpa,* translated "blessed fault," "fortunate fall," or "O happy sin!" The phrase derives from St. Augustine's famous allusion to one unfortunate event, the Fall of Man—Adam and Eve's fall and the loss of the Garden of Eden. The phrase is sung annually in the Exsultet of the Easter vigil: *O felix culpa quae talem et tantum meruit habere redemptorem*—"O happy fault that merited such and so great a Redeemer." The medieval theologian Thomas Aquinas cited this line when he explained the principle that God allows evils to happen in order to bring a greater good. The Catholic St. Ambrose also speaks of the fortunate ruin of Adam in the Garden of Eden by saying that Adam's sin brought more good to humanity than if he had stayed perfectly innocent. The concept also comes up in Hebrew tradition in the Exodus of the Israelites from Egypt and is associated with God's judgment. Although it is not a fall, the thinking goes that without their exile in the desert, the Israelites would not have the joy of finding their promised land. With their suffering came the hope of victory, and their life was restored. The term *felix culpa* can describe how a series of miserable events will eventually lead to a happier outcome.

For a while, Jack thought the name of this book should be *O Happy Sin,* so much did he relate to the idea. The very things that tripped him up—some inflicted against his will, some of his own free will, and some in between—turned out to be the gateway to grace and the discovery of new wisdom and life. *Felix culpa* seemed to him another way of saying that you learn from your initiations and the biblical stories of shalom and suffering, and these things make you into a far better person than you were before, in spite of what happened.

The greatest learning Jack discovered on the initiation weekends he led was how some of the young people experienced going under the dark, cold waters. They described the experience as akin to a place of abomination—an immoral, disgusting, or shameful place, according to the definition of the word. However, they explained how they felt strangely safe and at peace under the water. Some used the analogy of the womb—a safe, dark, watery place. They felt safe because they felt God was there. God was in the place of abomination. They had nothing to fear when they went down in life, for God was waiting for them. And surely, as the waters of baptism promise, they shall come back up again, changed and renewed.

Amazing grace! What a beautiful thing to happen—even sin made God's grace shine even more. The immoral, disgusting, and shameful place turns out also to be a place of grace.

Chapter Four

LOYALTY, LOVE, FAMILY, AND FRIENDS

*N*one of the grace Jack discovered would have been possible if it were not for the loyal love of family and friends. He is not sure if he can adequately put into words what that meant to him and how instrumental it was in getting his feet back on higher ground.

Again, there were one or two exceptions—but on the whole, his family and friends were rock solid alongside him. Not one family member faulted. A few friends did, but the majority were immovable. Coffee bars, restaurants, golf courses, kitchens, offices, TV rooms watching "the game," and family lounges became places of refuge and comfort. Endless conversations and hours of visits kept him going. Text messages, e-mails, phone calls, and cards kept his head above the water. Important days and holidays were always taken care of. He remembers one particular Mother's Day, of all days; he was spending the day at home alone when his brother insisted that he better get over quickly for lunch. Multiply that instance by a few hundred, and you get the picture. Their support was not just emotional but also in kind. They saw to it that Jack had no need. Sometimes he would stay over a few days, sitting quietly in the sanctuary of another home, where he could read books and leisurely spend time with others. He especially remembers staying up late four nights in a row watching the President's Golf Cup! Jack went on long night walks with the dogs, played hours of chess on the kitchen table, and played endless games of pinball and Tetris—simple things, actually, where small talk and friendship accomplished great things. There was many a long philosophical talk too, where much of what is written in this book was talked through in muddled and lengthy conversations.

How do you measure these things?

Jack couldn't measure this loyalty. It was gold to him.

Part Four

TO LOVE WITH JOY

"He lifts you up and he turns you around,
puts your feet back on higher ground"
(Van Morrison, "Whenever God Shines a Light")

Jack had once read that the secret of love is joy. He warmed to this idea, and though he had never known it in himself, he hoped one day he would. It had gone through his mind on several occasions what the key to this might be. Little did he know that the key to love with joy was suffering. He had never imagined that.

Chapter One

A NEW BEGINNING AT HOME

hough Jack knew the value of being alone in pain, it was not something he particularly liked. He had, however, over time, come to appreciate the aloneness and quiet that pervaded his life and was learning its value. He had learned much about loneliness and pain from a book by Henri Nouwen called *The Inner Voice of Love*, and it had become the rod by which he measured how he was doing.

> It is not easy to stay with your loneliness. The temptation is to nurse your pain or to escape into fantasies about people who will take it away. But when you can acknowledge your loneliness in a safe, contained place, you make your pain available for God's healing. God does not want your loneliness; God wants to touch you in a way that permanently fulfils your deepest need. It is important that you dare to stay with your pain and allow it to be there. You have to own your loneliness and trust

that it will not always be there. The pain you suffer now is meant to put you in touch with the place where you most need healing—your very heart. [9]

Jack had tried very hard to put this wisdom into practice in his life and felt, for the first time during his Honeydew experience, that he had succeeded. He was sure that was why something happened inside him, and he became better prepared for the future that lay ahead of him.

Of all the people who had stood by him, none had been so loyal and faithful as his son and daughter. Their time out at Honeydew was a wonderful bonding experience, and they all grew tremendously through it. Existing bonds of friendship and love deepened considerably. They would all come to look back at this time as most significant in their life journey together.

Another great influence at this time in life was the book *Ransomed Heart* by John Eldredge. Through his writings, Jack came to understand his life as an unfolding story. He also leaned to listen to his heart and to interpret the difficulties in his life as weapons of the enemy that sought to take away the heart life he shared with God.

And so he moved on and threw himself into the new church he was stationed in. He also enjoyed setting up home—just him and his son and daughter. These were fun and good times, and he felt renewed and excited about life and work again. He wanted his home to be a sanctuary, and it was. He spent hours sitting quietly, alone in his study, waiting and wondering what the future held. He was at peace and content.

He did question being in another suburban church, though. He felt a growing call within to the rural, less resourced church. He had never forgotten the missionary call that awakened in him in Namibia, and he hankered after such a challenge one day.

On one of those quiet days in the parsonage study, he remembered Stacy, a friend he had met some six years earlier on a spiritual retreat. She had invited him to speak at her church, and in the difficulty of his life at that time, he had let her down. He remembered her because she lived in the neighborhood he now lived in, and he thought he might bump into her as he went about his business in the town. His conscience worried him, too; he had never apologized, and he thought it high time he fixed that. So he called her, and after six years, offered a belated apology. Both their life circumstances had changed since their meeting six years previously, and so they decided to meet, renew their friendship, and catch up on the years that had gone by. They became good friends and enjoyed sharing together, discovering many common experiences and shared interests. Neither thought at the time that they would be anything other than friends, but as time went by, they realized how much they sought out each other's company, and the friendship developed into a committed relationship. They were both nervous about the "love" word and avoided it as much as they could. Jack, in particular, read all kinds of books on relationships and marriage, and they pondered over these things endlessly. Neither could make another mistake; the stakes were simply too high. Jack remembers finding a book which listed nine steps toward a healthy relationship. At their age, they were reading books on dating and relationships! They smiled and enjoyed the ride. He lost the book but remembered the nine steps. They were:

1. Mutual attraction
2. Friendship
3. Emotional safety
4. Trust
5. Commitment
6. Love
7. Marriage
8. Sexual intimacy
9. Long-lasting happiness

They hovered around points five and six forever!

Another bit of advice he picked up compared Hollywood love to real love:

Hollywood love:

1. Looks for the perfect partner
2. Falls in love
3. Marries
4. Divorces

Real love:

1. Strives to be the perfect partner
2. Chooses to love
3. Stays married

They also put their relationship to the test. They would listen to the people who knew them best—their family. If they got the green light from them, they would pursue the relationship; if they got the red light, they would reconsider their future. The lights were green, and they started talking about love and marriage. Jack was adamant he was not going to fall in love; rather, he wanted to be with someone whom he felt he loved and could commit to. In other words, he wanted his head to lead his heart.

In some way, they related to the biblical story of Job—they had also lost much of what they had and longed for blessing and peace in their lives. They adopted Job 42:12 as their own: "The Lord blessed the latter part of Job's life more than the first." They prayed for this and were determined they would do all they could to make it a reality.

Jack and Stacy decided over Christmas that they would marry at the end of the following year. Stacy had lost everything she owned in her divorce settlement and had decided to put in one last effort to recover that which belonged to her. Her divorce had been acrimonious. There had been threats on her life, her parents' home had been burned to the ground, and child support payments were few and far between. Jack was going to support her through the lawsuit, and they would get married when it was all over. In the meantime, Jack was corresponding with a friend and colleague, explaining how he hankered after a rural ministry but never got anywhere near it. One conversation led to another, and his friend pointed him toward a rural ministry in the Mississippi Delta in the United States of America. Jack and Stacy thought the Mississippi Delta was New Orleans!

They were about to be educated.

Chapter Two

A NEW BEGINNING AT WORK

*W*hile Jack longed for a new and different challenge in his work, he did not pursue anything intentionally. He made a few inquiries here and there, but that was all. He envisioned something in rural South Africa and wondered how he would ever get there. So when the Mississippi Delta came up, he was not sure how seriously to take it. Initially he thought the Delta was the New Orleans area, but when he discovered it was rural, farming America, his ears pricked up a bit. A rural ministry? A few months later, a call came through, and a move to a rural church in Mississippi became a reality. Jack immediately said yes, and a new chapter in Jack's life opened—not one he had planned or envisaged, but one which he gladly entered. He told Stacy he had accepted the position and told her he would come back for her at the end of the year to get married. But she wasn't having any of that. She decided to let the lawsuit go—a difficult and easy thing to do. It was difficult in that she felt justice had not been done, and easy in that she felt it was time to let the go of the past and move on with her life. She had lost everything, and Jack decided to leave all his furnishings behind. So they married, packed their few remaining possessions into suitcases, and crossed the ocean empty-handed to start a new life afresh. Jack realized that he had learned the initiation and biblical lessons. He didn't hold onto his life; rather, he let it go, and in letting go and having less, he found everything he had ever needed.

Leaving was not easy. Goodbyes were painful, but everyone—friends and family included—celebrated their love, marriage, and new life. Jack and Stacy left feeling that God had indeed "lifted them up, turned them around, and put their feet back on higher ground."

Leaving was also complicated in that threats had been made to prevent Stacy's two young sons from leaving the country, and a High Court Order had to be attained to give then permission to leave the country legally. That proved a costly and lengthy exercise, and combined with a nationwide strike that closed down the Home Affairs Offices, Stacy's sons did not get their passports or visas in time. Under threat of prevention to leave the country, they stayed in hiding a few weeks until their papers were ready, and they traveled to meet up with their stepfather and mother, who had gone on ahead as planned.

The promises of God held true, and they moved into their new life blessed and at peace. The lessons of initiation were now learned, the biblical stories validated, the grace of the church immeasurable, and the loyalty and faithfulness of friends and family repaid.

Life, blessing, trust, and peace all returned. Home and work flourished, and Jack and Stacy have yet to look back.

They love with joy now.

A deep sense of grace and gratitude permeates their lives.

Stacy and Jack had one more hurdle to jump. They thought leaving their country of birth and making a new life in another was nothing short of a miracle. They still wonder how it all happened—how all the threads came together and the challenges and obstacles were overcome. Their faith in God deepened. Only he could have done all of this. For them, it was impossible; but for God, nothing is impossible.

The hurdle came in the form of pancreatitis. Jack took seriously ill, and for a month, he lay in the University Hospital in Jackson, Mississippi, fighting for his life. Much of what happened was a blur in his mind.

He was really hit hard. The specialists told him, "We nearly lost you; you are a survivor—a miracle of healing." His sense of gratitude for being alive and healthy was overwhelming. He liked to listen to Kenny Chesney's hit song, "I'm Alive," and each time he listened, he gave thanks to God for the power of healing. He came to understand the power to heal is nothing other than the love of God at work—especially the love of a congregation, friends, and family. It was an outpouring of communal love that healed him. There was amazing faith all around; when his faith was lost and caught up in the tremendous struggle to survive, he discovered he could lean on the faith of others. But for him, it was as the apostle Paul wrote: "What good is faith that can move mountains if it does not love? There is faith, there is hope, and there is love, but the greatest of these is love."

Jack doesn't remember much of the days of October as he lay in the University Hospital in Jackson, but he does remember how he used to visit this dark and foreboding place and wonder if he would ever return. It was frightening. He went regularly to this place of suffering, pain, and despair. When he returned, it was as though someone had switched on a light, and he would look around the hospital room, checking that he was safe, sound, and okay. Many nights Stacy would sleep over in the ward with him, and he would ask her, when he called out in the middle of the night, to reassure him she was there, which meant he was there and had not gone into that dark and frightening place again. At first he thought he was hallucinating from all the morphine or just reacting psychologically to all that was happening. However, the longer he has been away from that time and the more he understood how thin was the thread his life hanged on, the more he began to wonder if these experiences were real experiences of the struggle between staying alive and losing his life. He sure had a sense that God was rooting for him and pulling him back from the abyss.

Some years previously, Jack had surgery to a broken ankle and developed a blood clot which shot into his lungs, and he suffered a pulmonary embolism. His one lung closed down, and a massive clot sat at the entry of the other lung. Should that clot move, he would not even know he had died. Thankfully it was thinned out through medication before it could do any damage, and Jack lived to tell the story.

Twice now he had come within a whisker of death. He lives now in constant gratitude to God for the gift of life. The words "thank you" are never far from his lips, and he feels a sense of joy in life he had never known before.

Life is no bed of roses, and Jack and Stacy still face many challenges and difficulties. Jack's illness brought with it a fair share of pain, heartache, and suffering. No one is immune to the things that unexpectedly happen every day, and Jack and Stacy still face uncertainty as every one else does—but they live with a deeper sense of thankfulness, praise, and reality than ever before.

Bibliography

1. Biddulph, Stephen. *Manhood.* Sydney: Finch Publishing, 1995 (222).
2. Fr. Richard Rohr
3. Fr. Richard Rohr
4. Fr. Richard Rohr
5. Fr. Richard Rohr
6. Fr. Richard Rohr
7. Fr. Richard Rohr
8. Fr. Richard Rohr
9. Nouwen, Henri. *The Inner Voice of Love.* New York: Doubleday, 1998 (47–48).

About the Author

Cecil Rhodes is a minister with the Methodist Church of Southern Africa on loan to the United Methodist Church of Mississippi, USA. He presently has pastoral oversight of two congregations in the Mississippi Delta—one in Greenville and one in Leland. He is married to Yviette and has two young adult children, Matthew and Robyn, two teenage stepsons, Marku and Leandru, and a new born grandson, Conlan.